# Symphonies of Theophanies

## Moroccan Meditations

# Symphonies of Theophanies

## Moroccan Meditations

Peter Dziedzic

First published by Pilgrim Songs Press 2016
Published by Lote Tree Press 2021
www.lotetreepress.com

Paperback ISBN 978-1-9162488-3-0
Hardback ISBN 978-1-9162488-4-7



Design: Rabiya Helle and Lote Tree Press

A CIP catalogue record for this book is available from the British Library

*To the awliyā', both hidden and manifest, who have guided me thus far.*

*To my teachers and mentors.*

*To the memory of Shaykh Hamza, Shaykh Ayashi, Sīdī 'Alī, and Ḥajjah Zulaykha.*

"To God belongs the East and the West. Wheresoever you turn, there is the Face of God. God is all-Encompassing, Knowing."

*Qur'an 2:115*

"There is no repetition in Divine self-disclosure."

*Shaykh ibn 'Arabi*

"The earth of Morocco lets saints grow in abundance like grass."

*ibn Qunfudh*

# *Contents*

# *Introduction*

The perennial human journey, one's truest vocation and the path to which innumerable sages and messengers have tirelessly called, is the path of remembrance. Remembrance is not an exclusively mental quality. It is a transformative element of human nature, the memory of rootedness in a Divine inheritance and of being with the One whom we knew before the act of knowing. It is the philosopher's stone of the mystics. This remembrance as spiritual matrix is known in Arabic as *dhikr* and it is the well-trodden way of the Sufis, the mystics of Islam. It is both activity and state, spiritual exercise and resting vision. As a practice, it is the recitation of Divine names, benedictions, prayers, Qur'anic verses, and verses of mystical poetry in the form of litanies. As a state, it is an attitude which seeks the Divine source in all things. As the Qur'an reminds, "Do you not realize that everything in the heavens and on the earth prostrates to God — the sun, the moon, the stars, the mountains, the trees, the animals, and many among humankind?"[1] It is a state of God-consciousness in which all creation participates and which we as humans are charged with bearing in and to the world.

Morocco is a land still imbued with this vocation of remembrance, of seeing and hearing the Divine praise and presence in all things. It is a country known endearingly by locals and visitors as *balad al-awliyā'*, the land of saints. It is a land which has nurtured the traditions of Sufism for over a thousand years, bearing the greatest luminaries of the Islamic mystical tradition in her womb, sustaining them with her fruits, and illuminating them with her radiance. The Sufis seek to bring humanity from states of forgetfulness and selfishness to an experience of Divine light. As *Shaykh* Aḥmad al-'Alawī, a famous Algerian Sufi saint of the twentieth century, once declared, "All the universe is Light. The only thing that darkens it is the manifestation of the self in it."[2] The Sufis seek to lift these veils of darkness, to be absorbed in the flames of Divine love, and to return, trailing those roaring flames as gentle candlelight, marking the way for all who seek the path.

[1] Qur'ān 22:18.

[2] As narrated by *Shaykh* 'Abd al-Raḥman al-Shaghouri and *Shaykh* Nūḥ Keller.

Morocco is a land of enduring beauty. From the intricate *zillīj* patterns and flourishes adorning the great mosques of the *medīnas* to the geometrical balance of the traditional Moroccan *riāḍs*, it is a place where a sense of the sacred is condensed into physical space and where the natural elements are consciously synchronized, allowing the earthly sphere to mirror the harmony and hierarchy of the heavens. From a simple steaming glass of sweet mint tea among strangers on the road to shared songs of celebration with neighbors on wedding nights, it is found in the warmth and hospitality of the Moroccan people. From the solitude of the desert to the stillness of the forests and the sea lullabies of the coasts, it is found in the glory of nature and manifested creation. To the vision transfigured, splendor radiates from all things.

It is a land of perpetual wisdom. Harbored in the words of living mystic masters both renowned and reclusive, the traditions of Sufism continue to pulse as the Moroccan lifeblood. Discovered in the Sufi lodges, the *zawāyā*, it radiates as a knowledge of the heart. Shared in the *masājid* and religious schools in cities and villages, it is carefully passed down as sacred knowledge from generation to generation. Hidden in the comforting encounters and sacrifices of strangers, it is revealed in unexpected moments of humanity. The wisdom of the Islamic tradition is cherished, protected, and embodied wherever one turns.

It is a land of continuous blessing. Known in Morocco as *baraka*, Moroccans believe in a Divine power imbued in the world which radiates from the *awliyā'* and holy places. It is the God-given grace, present at the resting place of every true master and channeled through the hand of every living guide, a blessedness which heals, aids, and gives structure to the world. It is found in grottos and springs, in devout prayer and sincere work, in generously offered cups of water and steaming tajines. It is a tangible, pulsating power nourishing the world.

This is a collection of various meditations from Morocco offering gleams of light and insight. Rather than discussing Sufi doctrine or religious history, I strive to paint portraits at the intersection of word and image, offering moments of reflection, stillness, and absorption. Each moment is a brushstroke of light, revealing a particular encounter with the *baraka* radiating in the *balad al-awliyā'*. Each instant — each encounter, thought, cry of longing, and breath — is a hidden theophany, a secret heartsong yearning for the heavens. This collection is a symphony of such moments, such heartsongs. *Symphonies of Theophanies: Moroccan Meditations* is a collection of poems, visual meditations with original photography, and tales of brief encounters carrying seeds of wisdom. Far from being a representation of the Moroccan tradition, this is merely a collection of my encounters, my attempt to share the beauty of the *balad al-awliyā'*. This land has hosted hundreds of seekers of sacred knowledge over the centuries, and a special few during my own sojourn. They, too, experience the *baraka* of Morocco in unique and blessed ways. This collection would not have been possible without their grace, humility, wisdom, and light on a shared journey.

Offered as an appendix is a glossary of Arabic terms used throughout. While I sought to avoid overbearing usage of foreign words, I chose to keep key terms which give life to the traditions and customs of Morocco. Many of these Arabic terms are quite difficult to translate, and many do not have a direct English equivalent. As this is not an academic text, I only offer enough to facilitate a reading experience.

I am indebted to all those I met in Morocco — to those who took me into their homes, to those who invited me to their gatherings, and to those who formed a spiritual family in Morocco. I am indebted to the *awliyā'*, who allowed me to sit among them and to take from their wells of *baraka*. It is in their honor that I share this work.

All error is mine, and all glory is God's.

*Peter Dziedzic*
*Fes, Morocco*
*March 2019*
*Rajab 1440*

بِسْمِ ٱللَّهِ ٱلرَّحْمَٰنِ ٱلرَّحِيمِ

## *Symphonies of Theophanies*

Symphonies of theophanies —
soft, subtle, immense —
emerge from each breath,
each heartbeat.
The Divine Names,
manifest, discerned,
explode in color
and patterns profound
and then dissolve into quiet
whispers, the depths
resounding in great
and simple glory.

# *Maqṣūra*

Within each atom
enrapt, attuned
to the chords of celestial spheres,
infinite lamps glow,
swaying,
aflame in deep
and simple
wordless
mantric
praise,
shedding light
in each crack
and crevice
of creation's song.
The source,
illuminating unicity,
blazes, pulsing
in each periphery
shadowed in veils
and vales, and,
if in each other
and in all things
we seek the distant embers
of those swaying,
praising
lamps,
memories stir
in the swirling mists of separation.
All things
become mirrors
of light,
all things
breaking

through brokenness
return
to the glowing
niche of fullness.

# *One Day*

One day
we will each become
a beautiful garden,
a windswept field,
forests
where capsules of cosmos
and universes explode in grass
and beetle and dewdrop,
painting great tapestries
of life.

## *Set Aflame*

Like a deer who yearns for living streams
whose lips have kissed the mountain brooks,
and like the love-drunk songs of sky-rapt birds
upon strung lyres of bewitched bards,
and like the dawn-kissed tree of life adrip
with wisdom's trickled quenching dews,
and like prophetic tongues enamored,
ablaze in luminous unveilings —
a dance bursts forth from atoms' secret
whispered roaring rites of love.
I am set aflame.

# *Known Through Simple Names*

A child with light-drunk eyes
gazes upon infinite seas
of wonder and mystery
known through simple names —
the quiet dances of candle flames
and slow streams of melting wax.

*Known Through Simple Names | Sīdī ʿAlī, Morocco | Offerings at the Tomb of Sīdī ʿAlī ben Ḥamdoush during the annual festival*

# *The Primal Vocation*

Our primal vocation,
a pre-eternal call,
the yearning of the *fitra* and
enchanted hearts,
a duty lingering
from a home long forgotten,
is the way of the alchemist —
crafter
and shaper,
poet
and lover,
transmuter
and sanctifier, charged
to carry the soul of the world
in fragile urns of mud
and glass
churned
from earthen furnaces
and to bear the secrets
of a language never fully
understood
at the isthmus of horizons.
Feet bound in clay,
our eyes turn to gaze upon
the vaults of heaven,
recalling covenants
which now seem
but distant doubt-rent dreams.
At the horizons intertwined,
the flowing font of all worlds,
we recall the obligations
of incarnation —
to mirror the heavens
in harmonious undulation
and to plant the roots

of the Cosmic Lote Tree[3]
in the fragments
of long-lost Edens,
to know the radiant songs
bursting forth
from each breath and cry
in the fabric of the world
spun upon the canvases
of Divine Names
and to see, in the soft trembles
and tremors of creation,
the wisps of glory trailed
from stardust into clay,
in the rites
and psalms
of intimate moments.
The alchemist's love flows
from the heart
as a pen drunk
on the ink
of a thousand wells
and breaks
through veils to see
a thousand lamps flickering
in scattered,
thundering darkness,
revealing the melody
of all creation —
whispers of what once was,
what is,
and what will be
once we recall the litanies
pulsing
at the confluence
of inner seas.

[3] The *Sidrat al-Muntahā*, the "Lote Tree of the Utmost Boundary," marks the end of the seventh heaven, which Muhammad crossed in his *Mi'rāj*, the "Night Journey."

## *A House of Knowledge, a House of Remembrance*

In the seaside town of Asilah on Morocco's Atlantic coast, I had lost my way looking for the seaside shrine of *Sīdī* Mansour, a local saint — a *walī*, as he was known in Morocco, a "friend of God." I turned a narrow corner and discovered the sea vista before me. Wandering the whitewashed maze of *medīna* alleys for nearly an hour, I grew weary. I rested on the walls of the Portuguese-built ramparts for a moment, admiring the view of the expansive sea before me. I walked out upon a long lookout pier jutting into the bay. At that moment, I turned to find the blue-rimmed dome of a tomb, the *ḍarīḥ* of *Sīdī* Mansour, arising from a rocky outcropping.

Waves crashed below in melodic succession. Several boys were scouring the rocks and shallow water below for scallops or other sea life to sell at the fish market. I sat absorbed in the sea breeze, the fresh scent of fish, and the sound of the lapping water. An old and hunched man ascended the ramparts and hobbled towards the edge carrying a bag of couscous. We exchanged greetings of peace.

"*As-salāmu 'alaykum.*"

He threw the bag of couscous onto the rocks below, the tiny spheres of wheat scattering in the wind like hopeful seeds.

"For the birds," he said.

"*Yā Sīdī*, is this the *ḍarīḥ* of *Sīdī* Mansour?" I inquired.

"Yes, it is."

"I would like to visit. Is it possible?"

"Of course, it is — I am the *muqaddam* of this place. I hold the keys. Come, come with me."

He took me by the hand and we made our way, slowly, to the locked, faded-blue door of the *ḍarīḥ*. He withdrew a ring of weathered keys from the folds of his *jellaba* and unlocked the door. We descended a flight of uneven stone stairs to the graveyard below. Carefully navigating the spaces between the unmarked graves, we made our way to the creaking door of the inner sanctum where the tomb of *Sīdī* Mansour was nestled, wrapped in green cloth adorned with Qur'anic verse. The room smelled of mildew and perfume, and straw mats covered the floor. Prayer rugs, cloths, rosaries, and books lay askew in all corners. The walls were caked in the same white and green paint as the rest of the complex, the faded hues revealing its age. The man sat in the corner, reciting *dhikr* with his prayer beads while I greeted the *walī* with the greeting of peace customary in pilgrimages to local shrines.

We then sat in silence for some time; the lips of the old *muqaddam* were aflutter with silent *dhikr*. I absorbed the sound of the roaring sea below and watched the sunlight play on the whitewashed walls. When the man was finished, we spoke. He had a warm face marked by deep blue eyes, a gentle gaze, a soft smile, and peeking grey whiskers. His name was Ahmed, and he had spent several decades as the *muqaddam* of this *ḍarīḥ*. When he learned about my studies in Fes, he smiled and reached for a box beside the tomb of *Sīdī* Mansour.

The wooden box creaked open and Ahmed retrieved a pile of yellowed pages from within. He placed it on his lap and began to sift through them. His eyesight had faded in recent years and he could not read the script. He asked to try my glasses, but they were of no use. He squinted, and once he discerned the first legible line, he began to recite the rest with ease and poured over one page after another. The pages were a dazzling assortment — old ledger sheets, torn pages from journals, receipts, cardboard, loose pages from books, printed workbooks, complete manuals, collections of poetry, and even pages from children's workbooks. Some of the ink seemed fresh while the rest had faded along with the paper. Some of the sheets were large, ornate parchments, and others were minute, illegible scraps. Some sheets were weathered to the point of crumbling while others bore the passage of the years with endurance. All of them, however, were covered in Arabic script written in the same distinct handwriting. Transcriptions of Qur'anic verses, prayers and *qasāi'd,* excerpts from exegetical treatises, and collections of sayings of the Prophet Muhammad graced the pages.

Ahmed rocked as he recited from the pages. He finished reciting a Qur'anic verse when he paused. He pointed to a corner of the room and asked me to fetch something from the ledge. It was an inkwell with three hand-carved wooden quills. I brought them over and he opened the ink, dunked the quill, and began a fresh page of text on the back of an ancient leaf of paper. It already bore a *qasīda* transcribed several years ago.

"The ink is made from the fish of this very sea," Ahmed said as he motioned outside.

With this inkwell and three worn wooden quills, he wrote volumes of leaves in this very room over several decades. He wrote for several minutes, but then went back to rocking and reciting. He seemed to no longer be in need of the text but was reciting from memory.
"From the page to your heart, *Sīdī*?" I asked.
"Yes. It is the only real way to learn!"

These were the texts he had memorized; the scraps of paper were merely the reminders. While he could no longer read the pages, the words blazed in his mind. I learned that between the prayer times, when he leads prayer at a local *masjid*, he spends his time at the *ḍarīḥ* reading sacred texts, writing, and praying. He motioned to another box, under a pile of clothes, which contained hundreds of other pages, stacks of writings from decades past. There were several such boxes scattered across the sanctum. This was a house of knowledge, a house of prayer, a house of remembrance.

"The waves, how beautiful they are!" Ahmed exclaimed after a moment of contemplation, "In all things is a reminder from your Lord. Do you not see? What is a single wave of this vast sea? It gathers, it crashes, and then it returns. All things return to unity."

He paused, smiled softly, and soon fell back into stillness and continued to recite. I told him of my intention to return to the *ḍarīḥ* of *Shaykh* 'Abdus-Salām ibn Mashīsh, the grandfather of the *Shādhilī ṭarīqa*, on Jabal 'Alam near Tetouan, one of the holiest sites in Morocco and North Africa, which I had visited with a group of companions the month before. Upon hearing this, he touched his heart and his eyes grew wide. He stood up and grabbed a stack of texts above the tomb, all composed by some of the greatest masters of the Islamic tradition — *Shaykh* Abu al-Hasan al-Shādhilī, *Shaykh* 'Abd al-Salām ibn Mashīsh, and *Shaykh* bin Sulaymān al-Jazūlī, among others. We poured over the texts, particularly the *Ṣalāt al-Mashīshiyya* of *Shaykh* 'Abd al-Salām ibn Mashīsh and the *Du'ā' al-Nāṣiriyya.*
"*Sidi,* when you return to the master, 'Abd al-Salām, do not forget to pray for me. That is a font of great *baraka.*"

We sat for some more time, absorbed in stories of the *awliyā'* of Morocco, especially the life and miracles of Sīdī Mansour. After an hour of stories and laughter, we faded into the stillness of *dhikr*, and I shared my intention to depart. Ahmed, with tearful eyes, gifted me a small text from the pile of worn pages — a collection of handwritten poems and prayers.
"Take the *baraka* of Sīdī Mansour with you, wherever you go."

We embraced, and Ahmed remained seated in *dhikr* as I departed the complex, offering a departing wish of peace upon the residents of the complex, both from this world and the next. The warm sun, the sea breeze, the din of the crashing waves, and the sound of Sīdī Ahmed's *dhikr* graced my departure. I made my way back through the maze of the old *medīna* of Asilah.

# *Patterns Hidden and Apparent*

Our earthly life is attuned to patterns both hidden and apparent. Which are hidden and which are apparent? Do we know, or is it but an illusion of knowledge? Are we ignorant, or is it but a lack of courage? There is a kernel of wisdom, a vision of discernment, and herald of holiness nestled within the cave of the heart. Nourish it and listen for it. It is the light that pierces the veils of separation.

*Patterns Hidden and Apparent | Fes, Morocco | A view of the minaret of the Bou ʿInānia madrasa from a rooftop*

## *Silence of the Heights*

Benedictions radiate from the tomb of the saint just a few meters away. "No one visits the tomb of a *walī* unless they are invited by the *walī*. It is written for you," pilgrims are reminded on their journey up the mountain. A guardian of the shrine sprinkles us with rose water as we enter the shrine. The silence of the heights is tempered by distant *qasā'id* of celebration carried on the wind, recited by pilgrims seeking the *walī's* blessings. There is *dhikr* in the hills, in the very stones and trees, joining the pilgrims' supplications in every moment.

*Stillness of the Heights | Jabal 'Alam near Chefchouan, Morocco | A view from the ḍarīḥ of Shaykh 'Abd al-Salām ibn Mashīsh*

# *Illuminating Wayfaring*

As you journey,
veils will be lifted.
Pearls of light descend
from friends both
hidden
and apparent.
Your pilgrim song is written
with each new revelation.

# *Music of the Spheres*

Shimmering mirrors,
the created planes
of stirring atom and string,
resound,
vibrating
litanies
reflecting
the incarnated music
of the spheres.

# *The Maps of Return*

The maps of return
are hidden
in plain sight.

*The Maps of Return | Fes, Morocco | A detail from the mausoleum Moulay Idrīs II*

# *Celestial Flower*

The cosmos is
a blooming celestial flower
unfolding
in each breath,
revealing the paths
of Heaven
as seeds of hope dispersing,
carried on the winds and tides
of the warp and weft of creation
to settle,
plant, and root
infinitely
manifest
blossoms
of life.

# *The Alchemical Song*

Haunt of scholars and
house of pilgrims,
    the sanctum stirs from slumber
    on a whispered autumn evening
as the call to prayer resounds
on ancient stone.
    The hawkers' cries fade
    into the fountain's trickling complaints
as the primordial tempos of
the alchemical song — inviting clay,
invoking spirit — emerges.
    Invocations of old stir and rise
in chambers of the heart, there
    where Adam treads
    and the Seal is enthroned.

# *At Their Feet*

The chants and prayers resound throughout the *zāwiya.* The stinging sweetness of the mint tea reminds us of the sweeter, truer taste of the evening, presence with the invoked Beloved. Scholars and students, united in a common song of the heart and spirit, sit together. Men of great renown are most interested in the simple questions of a new seeker of knowledge — a *ṭālib al-ʿilm.* Sitting at their feet, we seek in them the purest reflections of ourselves. They are lanterns in the darkness, voices in the night. The uncertainty, fears, and doubts of the outside world drown in a roaring sea of supplication.

*At Their Feet |Zāwiya Ben Souda near Fes, Morocco | A night of dhikr with fuqarā' and shuyūkh*

# *A Blaze of Dancing Light*

There is a blaze
of dancing light
in each atom's
song and
sway and
the only veil to this feast is
the blindness
of our sight, is
the soundness
of our certainty, is
the stirring cloud of fear
upon the mist of love-borne dreams.

## *Heartsong*

The way is long
            and I have wandered
far from well-known paths.
  The road to the sea
and the moon's light are distant
  in the folds of shattering night.
There is a cry
   of thirst,
       though silence
resounds
           and loneliness
breaks
       like a furious wave.
I pine for the path
     swallowed
        in veils of fog,
I yearn for the sea
whose veins
          into earth
       have dried
         and cracked,
I long for
  the kernel
of the kernel,
     that pearl
          of great price
       bartered for hollow shells
         at market stalls.
            Though I tremble
              before the deafening
                  rousing
              of a thousand
                  roaring

echoes
of distant faults,
the whispered wisdom of elders
and the memory of the promise
of love's effacing embrace,
cools like soft mist, reminding of
a lilt known deep within,
the cantos
and melodies
of a timeless litany —

*Birth*
*Longing*
*Ascent* —

a yearning
which seeks and sees
the tender glow of love
in all things.
To the depths and to the source, I am led,
by the turning
of the sacred mirror
in the caverns of our chest,
by the glimmering,
resplendent diamond
in the expanse of the mind,
and the trills
of that ever-new heartsong
at the core
of our being.

## *Springs of Prophetic Praise*

The *zāwiya* and graveyard were in an isolated corner of Fes, tucked away from the main thoroughfares and well-hidden from the main tourist routes and attractions. I was soon guided by the rising crescendo of melodious chanting. I stumbled through a twisted, rusted iron-wrought door and ascended the jagged stone steps leading up through the graveyard of Wazzānī *shurafā'*, an old and prominent lineage of Moroccan Sufis. I had reached the sprawling *zāwiya* complex of the Wazzāniyya brotherhood, or *ṭarīqa,* in Fes.

I ascended the steps and was welcomed by a group of old men swaying and chanting in unison. I was seated, promptly handed a glass of sweet mint tea and a piece of sweet bread — a nourishing gift and symbol of the spiritual *baraka* of the gathering — and was given a copy of the *Dalā'il al-Khayrāt,* one of the most famous prayer manuals of Morocco. I joined an age-old, enduring spiritual gathering of the Sufis of Fes.

A cornerstone of the Sufi way is the offering of blessings and prayers upon the Prophet Muhammad. Sufis have developed insight into the existence of the Prophet, his role as a universal messenger, and the metaphysical realities of his being. Sending prayers upon the Prophet is a Qur'anic injunction and a spiritual practice occurring at any moment all around the world. Most Sufis agree that in such an act are immense, incalculable spiritual rewards for those who perceive and understand the mysteries and subtleties of benediction.

On each day of the week, the *Dalā'il al-Khayrāt,* a collection of praises for the Prophet Muhammad, is recited — in part or in whole — in the city of Fes. A group of devoted old men of the *Shādhilī-Jazūlī ṭarīqa* have maintained this practice for generations. From Monday to Saturday, the text is recited as a group in a different *masjid* or *zāwiya* of the city, and it is often read by multiple groups at once. On Sunday, *murīdūn* of the *ṭariqa* read it individually, in the comfort of their home, so that all places receive the *baraka* of the reading.

The *Dalā'il al-Khayrāt,* a classic of the Moroccan spiritual canon, was compiled by the Moroccan spiritual master *Shaykh* ben Sulaymān al-Jazūlī. *Shaykh* al-Jazūlī came from the south of Morocco and studied in Fes, memorizing many important religious texts. He travelled in the eastern Islamic lands for many years and was later initiated into the *Shādhilī ṭarīqa*. Upon *Shaykh* al-Jazūlī's return to Fes, he wrote the *Dalā'il al-Khayrāt* after a miraculous event.

One day, the *Shaykh* awoke late for the *fajr* prayer. He stirred and hurriedly began looking for a source of pure water to make his ablutions, though none could be found. While searching, *Shaykh* al-Jazūlī encountered a young girl, who questioned the *Shaykh*. The young girl, aware of the *Shaykh's* conundrum, spat into a well, which began to overflow with pure, fresh water. *Shaykh* al-Jazūlī, astounded, inquired how the young girl attained such a high spiritual station. The young girl replied, in lovely simplicity, "I have done this by making constant prayer for God to bless the best of creation, the Prophet Muhammad."

Prophetic praise is the lifeblood of Moroccan spirituality, especially in the city of Fes. From the time of *Shaykh* al-Jazūlī's teachings, it has stood as a central pillar of Moroccan Sufi practice. In it, prophetic aspirations are embodied and the ways of Sufism come to life.

# *Two Celestial Domes*

The border between heaven and earth is a shimmering isthmus, the play of light and reflection, Source and radiant manifestation. Through reflection and refraction is one's form, one's destiny, and one's sanctity discovered and remembered.

*Two celestial domes | Rabat, Morocco | A view from the graveyard near the Kasbah of Rabat*

# *The Shepherd's Solitude*

On a late-autumn day, a shepherd tends to his flock in the pastures above the Middle Atlas city of Sefrou. The hills are silent, enveloped in a crisp breeze. The din of the city fades into the distance; only the soft rustling of leaves in the wind, a timeless bucolic ballad, emerges and soothes. We are at rest, warmed by the mid-morning sun and mountain air.

*The Shepherd's Solitude | Sefrou, Morocco | A shepherd with his flock in the hills outside of Sefrou*

# *Saints of a Different Order*

The first light of dawn broke through the sky, illuminating the distant, snowy caps of the towering High Atlas Mountains with a fiery orange glow. A pink-hued blanket of light spread slowly over the hills. Midelt, a town nestled at the eastern edge of the High Atlas Mountains, barely stirred in the early morning as the *adhan* for the *fajr* prayer sounded.

I travelled to central Morocco to visit the monastic community of *Notre Dame de l'Atlas*, a small community of Trappist monks. They made their home in a simple compound outside the village of Midelt. It was the first week of Lent, and I wanted to celebrate the new season with the Church. The weekend also marked the 91st birthday of Brother Jean-Pierre, a survivor of the Tibhirine monastic community, the majority of which was martyred during the Algerian Civil War when the monks chose to remain with the villagers. Jean-Pierre now calls Morocco his home. The story of the monks of Tibhirine had inspired me since my childhood and served as a testament to a lived and deep possibility of interreligious dialogue — a way of being in the world, a witness to unity in diversity, and a profound encounter of the Spirit in all things. I now had the opportunity to meet a survivor of Tibhirine, a living witness of deep, enduring faith and hope.

After arriving in Midelt, I had trouble finding the way to the monastery. I stopped and asked several locals for directions.

"*Ah Sīdī, As-salāmu 'alaykum. Fīn ṭariq ilā dayr, ilā al-ruhbān*? Where is the path to the monastery, the home of the monks?"

The question was unintelligible until, through explanation and gesture, my destination was understood.

"*Ah, al-Mirābitūn? Shuf.* Oh, the monks? Look." He pointed along a wide street that eventually wound its way over the hills to the monastery.

The word used to identify and name the men of *Notre Dame de l'Atlas* was not the traditional Arabic word for "Christian monks," *al-ruhbān* but *al-mirābitūn*, a name also used for the Muslim saints of rural Morocco who were known for their piety and their rootedness in a local community. The monks had also earned this title in the region. I had to ask for *al-mirābitūn* several more times, without confusion, before finding the entrance of the monastery.

The early morning light still crawled upon the horizon. I set off to join the community for Lauds and Mass, but I arrived at the monastery gates in the middle of the prayer. I did not want to disturb the routine of the ritual, so I sat outside and watched the spreading bath of sunlight upon the mountain ridge. The small monastic compound included a chapel, a guesthouse, and the living quarters of the monks. The entrance was flanked by two rows of beautiful trees which, in the heavy winds, swayed in tune to the cosmic Mass as the Eucharist was offered within the chapel. I sat under the trees in the stillness imbued with Divine Presence. I met the community after the Mass and was shown to the guests' quarters, where I would stay for several days. Though Jean-Pierre was resting after Mass, I was invited for a private meeting with the monk on Sunday.

While I joined the community for most of the Liturgy of the Hours, I also set aside some time for solitude, writing, and reflection. One afternoon, I walked through the countryside towards the High Atlas Mountains. Through dirt roads where children played, and over a river where women washed clothes and pots, and over hills where shepherds tended their flocks, I ascended a path which brought me over a ridge, leading to vast, rolling, and isolated slopes and planes split by a winding gorge. As distance grew between myself and the village, I became engulfed in a deep solitude. I approached the edge of the gorge and sat upon an overlooking boulder. The silence was marked by gusts of wind rolling down from the mountains. I remained here in contemplation for some hours, remembering the primacy of silence, and of listening, in the spiritual journey.

It is easy to fill one's time with spiritual activities, but often, to the distracted heart, these tasks become routine and rote exercises, dislodged from a firm root in mindfulness of the Beloved. Silence is essential for spiritual survival and flourishing, as is listening within the depths of that silence for an answer which springs from an eternal well, a truer memory. All of reality is a sign, a theophany in which a deeper Presence communicates. Silence trains hearts to be attuned to these moments. A unity emerges in the folds of a dazzling plurality, and in all things — in each sturdy rock and leaf fluttering in the wind, in each drop of water in the trickling stream below and in the darting swoops of the passing birds — this unity made itself known. My pilgrimage to *Notre Dame de l'Atlas*, too, was infused with a deeper Presence than I initially discerned. I was excited for my encounter with Br. Jean-Pierre.

That night, as the sun set and the deep hues of twilight returned, casting playful shadows upon the mountains, I returned to the chapel for Vespers, the evening prayer. As the psalms were recited, the *adhan* for *maghrib* prayer sounded from the village mosque, its gentle crescendo filling the chapel. The two invocations mingled, and the monks became silent in the middle of the prayer, allowing the melodious call to finish before continuing. Under the shade of the same mountain, the *masjid* and the monastery offered their sets of daily prayers to God, rooted in the deeper Presence I encountered in the hills.

On Sunday, I was invited to meet Jean-Pierre before lunch. I waited in the guest room, and as he opened the door and shuffled in, his face was marked by a glowing smile. He sat on the couch next to me and playfully rearranged the cap upon his head several times before settling into a solemn and welcoming stillness. The monk radiated a presence of peace. We exchanged some words of greeting and, after some discussion, I removed a *tasbīḥ*, a set of Islamic prayer beads, from my pocket. I purchased these prayer beads at the *mawlid* gathering of the *Qādirī-Boutchichi ṭarīqa* in Madagh the month before and, on Jean-Pierre's 91st birthday, I gifted him the beads — an exchange for the ways in which he and the entire community of Tibhirine inspired my journey across religious worlds. He accepted the gift with great thanks and we embraced.

Jean-Pierre is a living testament to the depth of joy that is possible in a life lived for others. Despite his hardships, despite losing his brothers to a brutal act of violence committed in the name of religion, Jean-Pierre bore his cross with grace, choosing to remain, choosing to love. He was a lamp that chose to remain in the world, a lamp which could not be extinguished. He was a flame that still had enough wick to flicker in the wind.

Before departing from the monastery, I spent some time before Compline, the monastic night prayers, under the rows of trees, staring up at the rich columns of stars shimmering in the deep-country sky. The calls for *'ishā',* the Islamic night prayer, and Compline sounded simultaneously, and at that moment a shooting star graced the firmament. It was time for Compline. The signs kept Heaven's time. I returned to the chapel for the communal recitation of the psalms.

My brief visit to the monastery had come to an end. I thanked the community for allowing me to welcome the Lenten season with them, and I promised to return for Easter. It was here, in the land of saints, that I encountered an unassuming saint, a living saint, a saint of a different order. The Moroccans had welcomed these monks as part of their own history, as seekers also rooted in the quest for God, worthy of the title of the saints — *al-mirābitūn.* As I left the monastery, the trees sighed and rushed in the wind, bearing witness to the unceasing theophanic symphony enveloping the hills outside Midelt.

## *Illuminations*

Illuminations
in the midst
of the mists
of night reveal
stories
of the worlds
praying,
the swirling heavens
swaying,
time's metronomes
flaying,
before the vastness
of the silence
of hearts engulfed
by mercy's promise
and love's
sweet rapture
on every fiber
of raw flesh
and brittle bone
and shattered dream,
before the vastness
of moments
where only tender
tendrils of moonlight
may enter
quietly,
fully,
with a whispered,
caressed,
heavenly
tincture.

# *Horizons*

Peaks
revealing horizons
revealing peaks
emerge, unfold —
inner thresholds
pierced, outer
limits fade,
a unity of horizons
is unveiled,
intertwined
in our gaze
on sun-drenched
skies.

# *The Lonely Tomb*

A storm rolls in from the north. The air drips with a chilled freshness as the earth longs for the soft kiss of rain. In the east of Morocco, on the road to Algeria, the tombs of *awliyā'* and scholars dot the countryside. They root in the plains and in the foothills of the Rif Mountains. This lonely tomb in the hills just outside of Mezguitem, the *qubba* of a local *walī* known for his piety, stands as a reminder of the sanctity of the earth and its inheritors. There is a stillness as the first drops of rain fall from the sky.

*The Lonely Tomb | near Mezguitem, Morocco | A marabout's tomb in the countryside near the Rif mountains*

# *The Primordial Wird*

The *ḍarīḥ* of *Sīdī* Shashkal graces the long stretches of Morocco's southern beaches. Fishermen visit the shrine early in the morning before commencing the day's work, and shells are left as a votive offering in exchange for the *baraka* of the *walī*. At high tide, the surf reaches the base of the tomb, and it becomes submerged in the sea. The lilt of churning sea waves and the bursting cries of seagulls, like a primordial *wird* of creation, leads pilgrims to a state of tranquility. The sanctity of the *awliyā'* becomes one with the sanctity of creation in the *balad al-awliyā'*.

*The Primordial Wird | Safi, Morocco | The ḍarīḥ of Sīdī Shashkal*

# *Light Upon Light*

Families gather to rest in the shade of the saint's home. The *zāwiya* of Moulay Idrīs II sits adjacent to the Qarawiyyīn *masjid* at the spiritual and physical heart of Fes. Moulay Idrīs II, a descendent of the Prophet who established Fes as a city of learning and worship, is continually venerated by devotees from near and far. Visitors come seeking the *baraka* of the saint and never leave empty-handed. He is the patron saint of the city of saints.

*Light Upon Light| Fes, Morocco | The sanctum of the zāwiya of Moulay Idrīs II*

# *The Tziddiq of Asjen*

The driver of the grand taxi, one of the typical worn, rusty, and decades-old though ever-enduring Mercedes-Benz sedans used for intercity transport across Morocco, sped through the bumpy road in the countryside near Wazan, a once-influential center of powerful Sufi *shuyūkh*. As we approached the village of Asjen, the driver slowed down near a long row of Moroccan flags set on a high wall and a pair of police officers stationed across the road. The driver slowed to a halt before a large gate and escorted me to the guardian of the cemetery before speeding off to drop off the rest of the other passengers heading home for the night. Following a swift registration process with the guardian, he closed his book and returned my papers, the formalities dropping in his wide smile and welcome. I was now allowed to enter and explore the Jewish cemetery of Asjen, home to one of the most important Jewish saints of Morocco.

Unknown to many, there is a rooted and enduring Jewish community in Morocco which claims a history stretching back centuries. Legends tell of rabbis who came to North Africa in the age of the Roman Empire and spread Judaism among the *Amazigh* tribes of the region. This created an enduring and indigenous Jewish culture of Morocco with unique languages, cultures, and traditions. Central to these communities is the veneration of the *tziddiqim* — righteous Jews who, like the Muslim *awliyā'*, are known for their spiritually, ethically, and intellectually rich lives, for various miracles, and for being models of holiness and fonts of blessedness.

The tombs of *tziddiqim* are scattered across Morocco. These holy men and women are often visited during the annual *hillula*, an annual festival honoring the life of the *tziddiq*. Several *tziddiqim* and *awliyā'* are mutually venerated by the Jews and Muslims of Morocco, an enduring legacy of the intertwined histories and destinies of these communities. I was here to visit such a *tziddiq*, the Rabbi Amran ben Diwan.

Born in Hebron, Rabbi Amran ben Diwan was an $18^{th}$ century rabbi sent to Morocco as an emissary of the Jewish community in the Holy Land. He settled in the city of Wazan and taught the Talmud for several decades. He acquired many students during his time and was known for his piety and wisdom. After his death, his tomb was visited by both Jews and Muslims. His grave was especially visited by those seeking healing from mental or physical ailments and women seeking aid in childbearing. Today, blessings of health and healing are still sought at the tomb of the Rabbi. The *hillula* of the *tziddiq*, where many gather to celebrate the life of the saint, was held in late summer. I came to join the festivities of the *hillula* and honor the life of the venerated Rabbi.

I walked through the graveyard, past several well-tended tombs, and approached the tomb complex of the *tziddiq*, a paved platform surrounding the grave of the rabbi. Rabbi Amran ben Diwan's grave was marked by a mound of large rocks, blackened by the flames of hundreds of votive candles offered over the years, and a massive tree, a symbol of the saint's continued, living presence. There was also a synagogue, a banquet hall, and several dormitories surrounding the tomb. Visitors of the *hillula* often stay for several days. I arrived at the end of Shabbat. Lights and a loud voice emanated from the banquet hall. I entered, was welcomed, and took a seat. A rabbi, a Moroccan Jew whose family had emigrated to France in the 20$^{th}$ century, was discussing the life of Rabbi Amran ben Diwan and the importance of the *tziddiqim* in the Jewish community today. Following the talk, I was introduced and welcomed.

It was a large and international crowd. Moroccans, French, Israelis, and Canadians filled the room. Almost everyone, however, had Moroccan origins, a snapshot of the Moroccan Jewish diaspora today. French was the primary language of conversation. Moroccan Arabic was used only among the remnants of the local Jews still living in the area. Morocco's Jewish population has rapidly dwindled since World War II and is in danger of disappearing within several decades.

After the discussion, we left for services in the synagogue. Prayers were offered as a community before visiting the grave of the *tziddiq*. The cherished tradition involves lighting candles at the grave and keeping the flame lit throughout the night, until the rising of the sun. Everyone was given candles to offer to the saint — sometimes lit individually or thrown all together onto the roaring mound of flames. The candle is a symbol of the living spirit and activity of the saint. It is an offering of one's own life, one's own light, to the saint.

As I sat near the grave, mesmerized by the blazing flames, I was approached by an old man who smiled and sat down next to me, offering me a cup of tea. I later learned that he was an Israeli scholar of Kabbalah, Jewish mysticism. He had a particular and lifelong devotion to Rabbi Amran ben Diwan, inherited from his parents and grandparents who would come to the *hillula* annually.

"Do you know who this man is?" he asked as we sipped our tea together under the tree.

Our faces were illuminated by the shifting shadows and roaring candlelight. We sat on a bench surrounded by devotees offering prayers and meditating. Several Muslim pilgrims, local villagers in Asjen and nearby Wazan, approached the grave and lit candles in honor of the *tziddiq* on the night of the *hillula*. I shared what I knew of the *tziddiq* and we entered a discussion of Judaism, Kabbalah, and the meaning of the *tziddiqim*.

"On this night, special blessings descend upon mankind and, in fact, upon all creation. The night of the *hillula* is a very powerful night. The channels of heaven are open wide for those who ponder them."

The *tziddiq*, like other holy and saintly figures throughout human history, occupies both earthly and heavenly realms. They are active on both planes, and thus seeking their support, particularly for the yearning supplicant, is beneficial for one's earthly and celestial destiny. The *tziddiq* is a bridge between the heavens and earth. Though both Jews and Muslims attribute all power to God alone, they recognize the importance of those who have already joined their Lord and the depth of their Divine witness.

"The *tziddiqim* are a door to our past and an inspiration for our future. What makes humans unique is their memory of something greater. Through the *tziddiqim*, our memories are sanctified. Through memory, we transcend ourselves. Memory is the portal to the sanctified life."

We continued our conversation for some time before the scholar left to complete his prayers and meditations at the grave of Rabbi Amran ben Diwan. The roaring mound of candles soon settled into a gentle collection of scattered, serenely swaying flames. People gathered around the grave throughout the night until sunrise and through the following day, speaking with old friends, sharing stories of the *tziddiq*, offering prayers, and sitting in silent reflection. I stayed the night and meditated near the tomb of the great *tziddiq*, blessed to share in this encounter with another Moroccan saint and to encounter other channels of grace and Divine remembrance in the *balad al-awliyā'*.

# *Minaret*

What need is there for a temple when all creation has been christened a realm of worship? For those with eyes to see, the whole world is a sanctified house of worship — each surface, a space of prayer, each structure, a minaret guiding the way to the heavens, inviting prayers and supplications at all times.

*Minaret | A "bayt al-jinn" near the Merzouga dunes | Merzouga, Morocco | A quiet moment before the rolling dunes*

# *Hillula*

A thousand prayers of hope
beat upon the eyes
as ancestral songs ascend
and memory's sweet rite
sustains the pillars of the world
in each moment.
Smoke climbs and
candles blaze softly long
into the stirring stillness
of the morning light.

*Hillula | Asjen, Morocco | The annual festival of Rabbi Amran ben Diwan on 1 Ellul*

## *The Shop of the Prophet*

Morocco brims, from sea to desert, with hidden saints, stories, and sanctuaries. For each well-known *zāwiya* or tomb, dozens remain hidden to even the sincerest of seekers. For each saint of great renown, a hundred hidden *awliyā'* populate the streets, markets, and *masājid.* The Shop of the Prophet, in the *medīna* of Fes, is such a hidden jewel despite its presence on the main thoroughfare of the old city. Forgotten by many locals, the story of the Shop of the Prophet is shared with those who are lucky enough to stumble upon a gathering within the small nook.

The tale is beloved to those who know it. The shop was once a *ḥānūt* — a place to buy daily goods such as food and cooking supplies. One night, the owner had a dream that the Prophet Muhammad entered his shop. The dream was vivid and stirred the owner from his sleep. He was absolutely transformed by this blessed encounter with the Prophet of Islam in the dream realm. Because of this vision, he closed his shop, emptied it, and sanctified it, transforming the small space into a *zāwiya*, a place for prayer, *dhikr*, and silent meditative retreats. He painted the new *zāwiya* exactly as he saw it in his dream — adorned with a deep, majestic green hue and rich *zillīj* patterns and flourishes. Though he sacrificed his career, he considered himself blessed to host the Prophet Muhammad in the imaginal and physical realms. He dedicated the space to the sanctification of human existence through the remembrance of God.

The *zāwiya* is rarely open. Those around the shop refuse to speak about it and several local shop owners even deny the story, a sign of strange times. It is open on special occasions during *Rabī' al-Awwal*, when the birth of the Prophet is celebrated. For those who are blessed with an encounter at the Shop of the Prophet, it is a special glimpse into a preserved pocket of Fes, one which seeks to sustain the spiritual lifeblood of the city and its special legacy of sending blessings upon the Prophet and practicing the remembrance of God. The Shop of the Prophet is just one of the hidden treasures of the land of saints, ready to be discovered by those who come with open, thirsty, and joyful hearts.

# *Memory*

Near the tomb of *Sīdī* 'Abd al-Malik in Kela'at Mgouna, an oasis south of the Atlas Mountains, lie the quiet, unstirring ruins of an ancient *Darqāwī zāwiya.* What once was a house of remembrance, hospitality, and healing has become a chamber of memories kept only by crumbling walls and shifting sands. Painted ceilings, resisting the passage of time in bursting glory, remain as a vestige available to visiting, wandering eyes. In the fading of memory, the beauty of transition and change remains, unfading. From the Divine Abundance all things come, and to it all things — all memories and quests and beings — shall return.

*Memory | Kela'at Mgouna, Morocco | The ruins of a Darqawi zawiya; details of a crumbling ceiling*

# *The Confluence of the Birds*

The conference of the birds
renews
in each age as
the hoopoe's cry rings
in each ear,
each heartbeat.

Though quiet, though
drowned in the swell of
infinite manifestation,
atoms moan and
yearn with
that great
aching outstretched plea for
fullness
and wholeness
and clarity,
the seal
of a primal covenant
|*Am I not your Lord?*[4]
known by its dancing shadows
upon spirits' eyes.
We are told:
|*Read!*[5]
Read
everything upon the land
and seas and skies
and in the depths of Heaven's vaults
and the fiery firmaments adorned
*read*
and remember.
In the ever-stirring conference

[4] Qur'an 7:172
[5] Qur'an 96:1

the confluence emerges
seeking springs of wisdom
pulsing, surging,
homecomings of
entangled roads revealing angels
borne on each breath of
the blazing phoenix
of the self-same flame as the
rooted Cosmic Tree.
|*Read!*
Read
that the straight path
is never straight
but curves and bends, the Face
and Names encountered ever anew
*read*
and remember.
The conference turns with
the *Simorgh's* blazing body built
in the swell of
birds of paradise
as a song rises from the growing din
and murmurs melt in unison
when echoes of moonlight resound
and the secrets of heart-caves whisper
and the chants of ancestral forest-halls recall:

*the ways of God are many*
*within this Sea of Mercy.*

|*Read!*
Read:
all the sages and their
journeys of life-giving taste
as the confluence rises, one

with the spinning cosmic spheres
*read*
and remember.

# *Threads*

Entangled
threads —
dances
faces
songs
embraces
stories
journeys
secret
soulful
prayers —
weave
memories
within minds and
dreams
among hearts,
binding
essences interwoven
blending
in bursting color
origins and trails
lost
amid time's short labors.
The tapestry
is unveiled
where threads reveal
vast patterns,
deep harmonies
to those who hold
to the tendrils
and quiet revelations
of the twisting filaments of moments
whose meanings cry out

to be known,
  and cherished,
    and remembered.

## *Mawlid in Madagh*

We set off on the road long before the early rays of dawn had graced the sky. It was the month of *mawlid* in Morocco. *Mawlid* gatherings, festivals commemorating the birth of the Prophet Muhammad in the Islamic month of *Rabīʿ al-Awwal*, were underway in Fes and across Morocco. Several students and I had been invited to attend the gathering of the *Qādiriyya-Boutchichiyya ṭarīqa* in Madagh, a small town near the Algerian border and the home of the *Qādiriyya-Boutchichiyya* community. We joined a caravan of *murīdūn* from Souq as-Sebt, a village in the south of Morocco, as they stopped in Fes to offer the *fajr* prayer.

A hushed prayer emerged from my neighbor's lips — the words rolling as gently as the passing hills. As the sun rose, so did the spirits of the *murīdūn* from Souq as-Sebt. Some would hum their *wird*, and eventually muted *qasā'id* emerged from the back of the bus. Before long, we paused at a rest stop. Sheets were laid upon the pavement for a breakfast of bread, honey, oil, and mint tea. I made a new friend by the name of Ahmed. Ahmed was finishing his doctorate in Sufi studies at a Moroccan university.

"Everyone who goes to Madagh finds something," he said as we sipped our mint tea, "You will find it hard to leave once your heart has been opened there!"

We commenced our trip once more; the rest of the journey on the road to Madagh was filled with the recitation of *qasā'id* — poems in praise of the Prophet Muhammad, of God's attributes and Names, and the Sufi path of wayfaring. The voices grew more intense and energetic as we went. As the bus sailed along the highway, I watched as the sun rose over the hills between Fes and Taza. The waxing and nearly-full moon cast its light upon the passing mountains and fields. The ethereal vista, the dance of shadows and shifting light on the vast expanses, grew more prominent as the sun rose.

We reached Madagh in the late afternoon; a large banner flew over the entrance to the village.

*The Global Meeting on Sufism : Sufism in the Contemporary Context.*

During *mawlid*, the *Qādariyya-Boutchichiyya ṭarīqa* was hosting both a *dhikr* gathering and an international conference on Sufism in the modern world. It was a confluence of scholars, pilgrims, and disciples. The bus trudged through the slow march of cars, bikes, and pedestrians filling the streets. What is normally a quiet village west of Oujda turned into a bustling center. We came to a halt in a lot filled with dozens of other buses.

*Murīdūn* had come from every corner of the country for the *mawlid* and to visit *Shaykh* Hamza, the master of the *tariqa*. The *murīdūn* from Souq as-Sebt pushed through the crowd to the pilgrims' lodgings near the main *zāwiya*. After we settled, Ahmed took me by the arm.

"Would you like to visit the *Shaykh*?"

I nodded and we immediately made our way towards the *zāwiya* and residence of *Shaykh* Hamza. The winter sun was low on the horizon, casting long shadows as we made our way through the throngs of visitors and *murīdūn*. We trudged uphill to the *Shaykh's* residence and were escorted to a long line to visit *Shaykh* Hamza. A somber silence fell between Ahmed and I as we prepared ourselves for an encounter with the *Shaykh*. The slow march through the hallway and stairway of the building heightened the anticipation. There was a slow crescendo of singing as we inched closer to the reception room. *Murīdūn* recited *qasā'id*, memorized and sung since childhood, in thunderous unison. We had entered the presence of the *Shaykh*.

I was greeted by a flurry of activity as several people crowded around and sang *qasā'id* in booming voices. Ahmed grabbed my arm and I turned to face *Shaykh* Hamza sitting on a couch and surrounded by *murīdūn*. The *Shaykh's* beaming smile caught my attention and lingered. He offered a gentle greeting as he welcomed me to the *zāwiya* for the first time.

"*As-salāmu 'alaykum.* Peace be with you."

He waved his hands in blessing over my head as our gazes met. Ahmed released his hand from my arm and clutched his chest. He closed his eyes and smiled. We made room for other *murīdūn* to greet the *Shaykh*. Ahmed did not speak. He only motioned to his heart with a sigh of relief and fullness.

A peaceful stillness surrounded us as we left the *Shaykh's* quarters and walked through the exit and through a small garden and cemetery. Ahmed could not speak for some time. We paused at the tombs of *Shaykh* Hamza's ancestors — luminous figures and previous *shuyūkh* of the *Qādiriyya-Boutchichiyya ṭarīqa.*

"When you meet your *shaykh,* your heart sings," Ahmed said, breaking the silence.

The din of the village returned — the honking of distant taxis, the chanting of *qasā'id*, vendors' cries, the giggles and squeals of children, and birdsong. The chatter seemed new, symphonious, with refreshed clarity after the encounter.

"It is the only real connection you can know in this world," Ahmed continued.

We stopped for a moment at the top of the hill to enjoy the sunset over the golden fields, ablaze to the edges of the horizon.

"Whoever remembers God, God is present with them. They are a Divine window. This man is always remembering God. We always have a window to our Lord."

As the call for the sunset prayer sounded, we made our way to the main *masjid* of the expansive *zāwiya* complex.

"Sufism is not a garb. It is the science of reality itself. If your mind and heart are not unified, then you have not found your way."

The *murīdūn* entered the *masjid* slowly, enveloped in conversation with one another. We moved through the growing crowd and sat in a corner of the *masjid.* Many brought blankets and were wrapped in thick wool *jellābas* as the biting desert cold emerged with the setting of the sun. They came prepared for a long night. Recitation began, and several *murīdūn* from Souq as-Sebt and Fes sat together. I sat next to *Sīdī* 'Abd al-Ḥaqq, an Arabic teacher from Fes. We looked at the crowd huddled together before and behind us.

"There is a difference between scholars and *awliyā'*, the friends of God," Abd al-Ḥaqq shared as *murīdūn* passed around glasses of tea at the start of the *mawlid,* "A scholar's quest is knowledge. That is important. A *walī*'s quest is for intimacy. That is essential."

The singing of *qasā'id* grew louder with each passing moment, signifying that the event was about to start. *Shaykh* Hamza entered the room and took a seat in the center with several other senior officials of the *ṭarīqa* and visiting guests.

"The *Shaykh* does not write any books. All of us, our lives and hearts, are his books — books of life!" 'Abd al-Ḥaqq said, laughing joyfully as he took a sip of tea.

The *mawlid* began with the famous words of the *Qasīdat al-Burda*:

*My Lord, confer blessings and peace continuously and eternally on Your Beloved, the Best of All Creation…*

The *mawlid* in Madagh continued long into the night, filling the hills with prayer until the early hours of the morning.

# *Crystal Empyrean*

Gazing heavenward, new worlds once unnoticed reveal themselves in patterns intricate and profound. Worlds within worlds bloom eternal — ever-fresh, ever-new, ever-alive. Creation unfurls outstretched, yearning always for the heavens above and within. In the all-encompassing gaze, we rediscover holistic vision. We recover the cord of remembrance leading back to the center.

*Crystal Empyrean | Alhambra, Granada, Spain | Detail of a ceiling*

# *Celestial Trails*

During a *ziyāra* into the hills above Meknes to visit the tomb of *Sīdī* ʻAlī ben Ḥamdouch, the sun breaks through the storm clouds, illuminating the countryside on a late-winter evening. Morocco, the land of saints, is steeped in *baraka,* in a blessedness of abundance both manifest and concealed. It is the firm conviction of the local pilgrims who visit the tomb of the *walī.* Such a vision demands seeing everything anew, alive, for the very first time.

*Celestial Trails | Sīdī ʻAlī, Morocco | The sun breaks through the clouds after a rainstorm in the hills above Meknes*

# *The Land of Saints*

O, Land of Saints,
may every atom
ever bleed
sanctity.

*The Land of Saints | Ait Bougamez Valley, Morocco | A view from above*

## *Saints of the Open Road*

While travelling in the south of Morocco, I visited a friend in Ourzazate, the capital and hub of the region south of Marrakesh and the High Atlas Mountains. We were interested in exploring the region together and decided to head south through the Draa' Valley. The Draa' river, Morocco's longest waterway, dissects the valley and a string of *kasbahs* and oases lead travelers to the edge of the Sahara. Our destination was the *Nāṣiriyya zāwiya* of Tamgroute, a place of historic and contemporary pilgrimage at the southern end of the Draa' Valley and one of the final outposts in Morocco before the Saharan expanse and the Algerian border.

The *Nāṣiriyya ṭarīqa* was once one of the largest and most influential Sufi orders in the region. Though the valley and village were centers of religious learning and spirituality for centuries, the *zāwiya* of Tamgroute was founded in the 17$^{th}$ century by *Sīdī* Muḥammad ibn Nāṣir al-Drawi. He cultivated and spread the teachings of the *Shādhilī ṭarīqa* across the Maghrib. The *zāwiya* developed into an important Qur'anic *madrasa*, attracting students from far and wide.

Through the travels of *Sīdī* Muḥammad's son, Aḥmad ibn Nāsir, the *zāwiya* cultivated one of the most important manuscript libraries in North Africa, amassing manuscripts and volumes from across the Islamic world. Today, the vast collection remains well preserved in the dry desert air. My pilgrimage to the *zāwiya* was one of both mind and heart, to a center where the intellectual and spiritual sciences were cultivated and united in the seeker's quest for wisdom and understanding. We set off in a battered, though sturdy, rental car in the early morning, renewing our intentions and excitement. We hoped to reach Tamgroute by sundown and participate in a *dhikr* gathering at the *zāwiya.*

It took us several hours to cross the mountains into the valley. There was a beautiful and jarring contrast between the green of the valley oases and the rugged, barren mountains and deserts surrounding them. The oases trailed the Draa' river like a string of pearls. Beyond the occasional *kasbah* and village, long stretches of barren road filled the horizon. Soon, nondescript structures began to dot the road south. They were *qubbas*, the tombs of the local *awliyā'* of the valley. These domed structures are built to mark the graves of locals renowned for their sanctity and piety. There were many to visit along the way. At each structure, we decided to stop, visit, and pay our respects to the local *walī*, often situated at the center of a modest and obscured roadside graveyard. Some *qubbas* were well-kept while others were crumbing and destroyed. Some hosted local visitors, and others were deserted and vandalized, the tombs desecrated and raided. Often, it was impossible to determine the names or stories of the *awliyā'*. There was no remaining testimony to the life and work of the *walī* other than a simple earthen mound with an erect, unmarked wooden plank as a gravestone. The *qubba* was often at the center of a graveyard, a field of mounds marked by a few stones. The simplicity of these tombs, in stark contrast to the intricate urban tombs of famous *awliyā'* such as *Moulay* Idrīs II, *Shaykh* Aḥmad al-Tijānī, and the *shurafā'* of Wazan, embodied an oft-recited mantra of the spiritual path — we are all equalized in death; we are all equalized before our Lord.

The tombs of these *awliyā'* popped up like desert oases on the long road. We stopped at each *qubba* along the road, a font of *baraka* renewing our intentions and joy. Greeting each *walī* seemed a necessary duty sanctifying our path south. We reached Tamgroute by evening, our pilgrimage sealed, blessed, and guided by the saints of the road. The next day, we explored the collections of the library, pouring over beautifully illuminated manuscripts and joining the local community in prayer and remembrance. The pilgrimage of both mind and heart was successful.

The presence of the *awliyā'* spans Morocco from east to west; some were great, world-renowned spiritual masters, others were district legal scholars or village Qu'ran reciters, and others still were individuals known for their simple piety or charity. The tombs across Morocco stand as memorials of communal memory, flickers of a past sanctified by men and women of the spiritual path.

The tombs dotting the road on the way to the *Nāṣiriyya zāwiya* were a testament to the Moroccan legacy as the land of saints, the *balad al-awliyā'*. This legacy is rooted in the visitation of these *awliyā'*. Their memory is maintained not only in the practice of *ziyāra*, but also in the circles of *dhikr* and Qur'anic recitation across the country. The Moroccans I encountered often attributed the relative safety of their country to the constant recitation of the Qur'an and the Divine Names across Morocco — from desert to forest to coast. The tombs of these saints, and the maintenance of their memory through visitation and supplication, are another enduring testament to that celebrated, remembered, and cherished religious inheritance of Moroccan Sufism.

## *Ghosts of the Medina*

As the *adhān* for the sunset prayer sounds, the once quiet alleys of Larache stir to life. Feet shuffle, trees rustle, and the sound of distant waves crashing upon the shore join in a clamorous melody. The memory of the city, too, stirs. The same call that has sounded for hundreds of years repeats once more, invoking a different order of time.

*Ghosts of the Medina | Larache, Morocco | A public square at dusk*

## *Silence*

Its ways are known to those who
long ago dispensed with the burdens
of names and faces and yet still swoon
before each heartsong's plea to know
true Names, the luminous Face of each
wayfaring pilgrim upon the road, to gaze
upon the knotted tendrils of atoms
imbued with transcendence.
It is known in silence,
haunt of ancient intuition,
womb of wisdom
and all creation.
From silence trembles forth
vibrations, cosmic pillars,
primal waters bearing sound,
song, and the Word
once known as soft
flickers of fullness found
in hidden moments —
a mother's caress
in the depths of night
and sorrow's sting
at life's first aging flutters,
hymns of new hope etched
on hearts and storm-kissed horizons
and the lingering heat of love's first
effacing embrace.
A foreign fullness,
an unfamiliar, distant,
awfully brilliant abyss calls.
We stumble, tremble
toss and turn rapt
in the terror of loss

as false forms melt away
as wafting smoke
before memories of
celestial longings fulfilled,
where eternity breaks forth
and passes again, a token
of the journey forgotten,
broken
by the recollection of
separation.
Fast from words,
and stillness is found.
Bathe in stillness,
and the Word is found.
Drown in the Word,
and words seem
but parceled prison cells
of singing, stirring souls.
The language of hearts is rediscovered —
always known, merely forgotten
for a moment upon the road —
and traces the paths
of the pilgrims' dance
to the nameless, tuneless
songs of silence.

## *The Zawiya is Everyone's Home*

I sat in a small café in the village of Erfoud and waited for the shared taxi van to fill and begin its route westward towards Tinjdad. I spent the previous week visiting several Sufi communities in the south of Morocco. After visiting a small, *Darqāwī*-owned farm near Oukeet, I learned of a nearby *Darqāwī zāwiya* in the village of Touroug. I intended to visit and spend time with the community of *fuqarā'* at the *zāwiya* before continuing to the renowned Qur'anic school of Tizguarine.

I sat in the café for several hours, nursing a sweet Moroccan tea while watching the dust race around in the wind. It was early April, and the southern heat was a welcome change from the lingering late-winter chill of Fes. As I waited, I noticed a young, well-dressed Moroccan man take note of me from across the café. After the last trickle of sweet Moroccan tea had dried-up in my glass, and after I had finished translating an Arabic text while keeping track of the number of *ḥajjahs* climbing into the van, I turned to the man and smiled. He stood and walked over, sitting down beside me.

"*As-salāmu 'alaykum. La bās*? Peace be with you. Are you well?" The man offered.

"*Wa-'alaykum as-salām. Bkheyr, Alḥamdulillāh. Wa anta*? And Peace be with you. All is well, thanks be to God. How are you?" I returned.

He took a seat, and we began our conversation. His name was Mohamed, and he was an accounting student in Errachidia. He was returning to his home in the village of Tamellalt on holiday. I explained that I was visiting the *Darqāwī zāwiya* of Touroug.

"I will come with you, if that is ok. After that, you will come to my house."

I was a bit startled at his self-invitation.

"Thank you *Sīdī*, that is truly kind of you. However, I intend to spend the night at the *zāwiya*, and then continue to the Qur'anic school of Tizguarine. I already told them I was coming."

"Ok, no problem. I will still come with you! You are a guest and friend."

I did not tell the *zāwiya* I was bringing any guests, and I thought it might be poor *adab* to show up with an unexpected guest who expected food and a bed. However, out of respect for my new friend's hospitality, I did not protest. The grand taxi was nearly full, and the driver honked his horn to summon me. Mohamed grabbed my arm and wrapped his around mine.

"Welcome to our home!"

The van sped westward towards Tinjdad. Storm clouds gathered on the horizon and were moving towards us. We met the encroaching storm halfway down the dusty road. Heavy rain began to fall. The van was full to the brim, and Mohamed and I stood, our necks curved, as the bus rattled along the broken road. The din of hushed conversation and rain on the metal roof was broken by Mohamed's questions. He was excited to have a foreign friend and practice his English. He was honored to have a guest visit him and his family in their village. I, too, was honored, but I was also worried about upsetting my hosts at the *zāwiya*. Mohamed assured me that it would not be a problem.

We arrived at the *zāwiya* of Touroug and dashed from the van, seeking shelter from the rain. I approached the door of the *zāwiya*, hidden behind several buildings, and rang the bell. Several moments later, an old white-bearded man opened the door and walked us to the *zāwiya*. We were quite late due to the storm. We took our shoes off, entered, and greeted the men sitting on the floor with a kiss on the hand, beginning from the right. One of the *murīds* went to the corner and prepared a kettle of tea on a small stove.

I found my mind engulfed in worry as the thunder roared and rain pounded against the windows. Were they upset that I was late? Were they not expecting my guest? Did I do something inappropriate? Mohamed sat next to me quietly, smiling. The old man who welcomed us returned with two cracked wooden bowls filled with *ḥarīra*, which Mohamed and I ate together.

I watched as the man in the corner prepared the tea with diligence — piling blocks of sugar into the warming kettle, pouring the tea into glasses to mix the sugar and leaves, and tasting it with a smack of the lips to confirm its sufficient sweetness, a rhythmic art of the *zāwaya.* After distributing the tea, the men began to chant a *qasīda* from the *dīwān* of *Shaykh* Muḥammad ibn al-Ḥabīb. Soon, the call for prayer was sounded from the nearby mosque, and the men scattered to make ablutions and prepare for the prayer. Mohamed and I were left alone in the *zāwiya.*

"Mohamed, I did not tell them I was bringing a guest to spend the night," I said in turning to him. "I am worried they are upset with me."

"Do not worry, my friend. It is not a problem."

"I think it is poor *adab* to bring a guest unannounced, Mohamed. How can you be so sure?"

"When I was a child, we would always go to the *zāwiya* for these things! To eat and rest and make *dhikr.* I would go with my family and I would go with my friends. This is the work of the *zāwiya.* The *zāwiya* is everyone's home!"

After he spoke, I paused and reflected. I was allowing my foreign standards of hospitality, communication, and community to affect my interactions at this *zāwiya* and with Mohamed. In the south of Morocco, *zawāyā* play an important social role, and unexpected guests are often housed and fed without notice. The *zāwiya* was indeed everyone's home, a place of rest and prayer and reflection for every traveler on the road. I apologized to Mohamed for my misunderstanding.

"Do not worry, my friend. You are our guest!"

The men slowly reassembled for the prayer, and the rest of the evening was spent in *dhikr,* singing the *qasā'id* of *Shaykh* Muḥammad ibn al-Ḥabīb, a beloved master of the *Darqāwiyya.* We slept in the *zāwiya* as the storm continued, softer.

In the morning, we sat with some of the men, eating *ḥarīra* and drinking Moroccan tea. After chatting for some time, Mohamed and I had the opportunity to visit the adjacent tomb of the *Darqāwī walī, Shaykh*

Muḥammed Bel Qurshī. We offered our greetings and prayers and sought the *baraka* of the *walī* before parting ways with the *muqaddam* of the *zāwiya.*

Mohamed and I were on the road again, heading towards his village. I was ashamed that I had doubted the hospitality of the Sufis and of the *zāwiya.* I left, however, with a renewed sense of humility. I now had a new and patient friend with Mohamed. We spent the following day together, enjoying the countryside after a rejuvenating night in the *Darqāwī zāwiya* of Touroug, one of my many new homes among the Sufis of Morocco.

## *Transfiguration*

The borders
between shadow and
light,
poison and
salve,
fear and
faith,
are thin
wispy
veils
masked
as looming towers
and misty canyons
and forest thickets
in moments of doubt,
of whispering despair.
The source
of our greatest promise,
and the spring
of our truest Name
bleeds
into shallow veins
where we think ourselves
greater than our self,
where envy drowns deep
wells of gift
in hearts
that have not been healed,
caressed,
blessed,
transfixed
by that great love song
which holds the cosmos

on gentle pillars
of wind and water,
of promise and trust.
When our hearts have been
rooted, our vision,
transformed,
our minds, transfigured,
our selves,
bathed in the grace
infusing all moments,
the dark veils
known as shadows
will be lifted, revealing
the great lamps
that always were
and our truest Names
known
as One.

## *Beatific Vision*

O children
of unified sight,
O sons and daughters
of each passing age,
*Yā ibn al-waqt*[6]

seek always
the Whole,
the radiating,
pulsating
beatific vision
shining
in all things,
and it shall envelop you
in the same sacred fire known
in star cores
and Lote Tree boughs
and prophetic pauses
and enamored
enflamed
hearts.

[6] "Child of the Age," a common title for a Sufi.

## *Baraka*

Each
wayfarer
on the road
and each
pilgrim
in the throngs of prayer
seeks those sacred
subtle blessings
that enchant and heal our
fallen frail atoms —
supplications
invocations
petitions
pleas
and chants
legend and tale
and sweet succinct memory
have named the wells
where grace springs
and breaks upon the weeping world,
yet for the traveler
transfigured
the ink of the Names
paints the canvas-world
in infinite
mysterious
glorious
strokes
and all the worlds manifest
the gushing spring,
the font of life.
The whole earth reveals
a vision of the heavens,

creation radiantly redeemed,
        radiantly glorious.
The way
        is in the vision,
          transfigured.

# *Impermanence*

A portal to the ruins of an ancient *Darqāwī zāwiya* in Kela'at Mgouna. The house of remembrance maintains its purpose for visitors of pure intention and reflection. In the ruins of this sacred house reside reminders of impermanence, the destiny of temporality, and the glory of a hidden ascent. In the crumbling stone and rotting wood, the path of transcendence has been made clear.

*Impermanence | Kela'at Mgouna, Morocco | The ruins of a Darqāwi zāwiya*

## *The Moussem of the Perfect Master*

I wandered through the winding alleys of the Meknes *medīna*, performing *dhikr* for several hours after a visit to the *zāwiya* of the *Darqāwiyya-Habībiyya ṭarīqa*. As I neared the edge of the *medīna*, a din arising from beyond the city walls grew more pronounced. I emerged from one of the *medīna* gates and stood before a sprawling street market stretching into the distance.

The streets were lined with dozens of tents, their luffing white canopies reflecting the strong late afternoon sun. The passageways thronged with families, children, vendors, and animals, and the scent of charred meat and smoke from the grills filled the sky. I looked up the hill, past the sea of people and maze of tents, towards a glimmering green sloped roof — the *ḍarīḥ* of a *walī* of Morocco. I made my way through the market and up the hill to greet him and fulfill the intentions of my *ziyāra*. It was the eve of *mawlid*, the birth of the Prophet Muhammad.

In the Islamic month of *Rabīʿ al-Awwal*, Moroccan homes, *ḍarīḥs*, and *zawāyā* burst with life as families and communities come together to celebrate the birth of the Prophet of Islam. Festivals and gatherings take place across the country throughout the month. It is also customary to visit *shuyūkh,* the bearers and sustainers of the Muhammadan light, during the month. After attending several nights of prayer and *dhikr* in Fes, I was invited to the *moussem* of the *ʿĪsāwā ṭarīqa* in Meknes. Annually, the *Īsāwā* gather at the *zāwiya* of their founding *shaykh,* Muḥammad bin ʿĪsa, in Meknes to seek his *baraka*. People spend several days in the *zāwiya*, sleeping among the tombs, seeking the *baraka* of the *walī.*

I entered the maze of tents and made my way up the hill. Erected for the *moussem*, the tent city housed the visitors and pilgrims who could not find a place to sleep in the *zāwiya*. Hundreds of people had gathered from across Morocco and the region to visit their *shaykh* on this blessed day. Several of the tents hosted gatherings where people were chanting, playing instruments, and falling into trance during the *laila*, a nighttime ceremony. I continued through the tent city towards the *ḍarīḥ*.

*Shaykh* Muḥammad bin 'Īsa is a popular Moroccan saint. A master of the *Shādhilī* order, Muḥammad bin 'Īsa was known as *Shaykh al-Kāmil*, or the Perfect Master. He was a benevolent *walī* and spiritual guide who reflected the mercy and wisdom of the Prophet Muhammad, the vocation of every *shaykh*. His tomb graced the top of a hill at the edge of the Meknes *medīna*, where a sprawling cemetery grew out from the tomb's location over the centuries.

The chanting of *dhikr* could be heard emanating from the tomb above. I continued my ascent along with dozens of other pilgrims. The spirit of the *moussem*, the spirit of pilgrimage, is the lifeblood of Morocco. The promise of *baraka*, of intercession, favor, and healing, beckons to those who seek the fonts of Divine grace.

The entrance to the tomb was marked off by metal barriers. There was a long and winding line to enter the *zāwiya*. Slowly, we made our way into the tomb of *Shaykh al-Kāmil*. The intricate *zillīj* patterns of the sanctum shimmered in the sun. Every inch of the *zāwiya* was covered with straw mats, blankets, pots and pans, piles of bread, and small stoves for tea. Visitors shuffled in a narrow line to visit the tombs of the *walī* and his companions.

I finally reached the tomb, where I offered a greeting of peace to the *walī*. Devotees and descendants of the saint sat gathered around the tomb, offering prayers on behalf of those who came with special requests. A group of *fuqarā'* began to recite vociferously from the *Dalā'il al-Khayrat*, their bodies swaying in sync with the others who offered their prayers to God before the tomb of *Shaykh al-Kāmil*.

*O God, send Your blessings and peace upon our master, Muhammad, and upon his family and companions.*

After spending an hour in prayer in the *zāwiya*, and after receiving a blessing from the descendants of Muḥammad bin 'Īsa, I left, allowing others to visit on this blessed occasion. The sun was setting on the horizon, and the *adhān* was about to sound. *Qasā'id* reverberated in the halls of the *zāwiya* throughout the night. I made my way through the street market once more and stopped to share a cup of tea with a family from Marrakesh. They made the long, cross-country trip to pay their respects to the honored Moroccan *Shaykh*.

"We have been in the *'Īsāwā ṭarīqa* for generations, and the *moussem* of *Shaykh al-Kāmil* holds a special place of honor for our family. You were blessed to have been called to visit on this special day!" the father said as we shared our tea.

The festivities would continue throughout the night and pilgrims would visit *Shaykh al-Kāmil* over the course of several days. I returned to Fes that evening, carrying the *baraka* of *Shaykh al-Kāmil* in my heart through the rest of my stay in the *balad al-awliyā'*.

## *In Praise of the Most Praised*

The ways of the masters are recalled
renewed in
roaring, whispered prayers
unfurling memories,
piercing cosmic veils,
revealing ancient yearnings:

O, Song of Fullness,
Ring, ever tender, ever subtle,
upon those seeking the inundation
of gentle dawns and still, silent twilights.

O, Gnostic Elixir,
pour forth from celestial horizons
soak the raw, red earth
in forgotten promises of transcendence.

O, Road of All Yearning,
wind through brittle hearts, and quench
where thirst sinks to primal roots,
and remind of Love's sweet dewdrops.

O, Mercy of the Universes,
speak always in the tongues of all sages
and reveal the ways of Unicity's wisdom,
the words of first covenants.

O, Most Beloved,
may your praise forever fill those hearts
turned to your shimmering manifestations
and bowed before descending graces.

May the Loved of the Beloved always
sustain us as the People of Burning Love.

## *Seeking*

I will speak to you,
O Beloved,
in all my native tongues —
awe
before the twilight canvas
and private sojourns
in forest brambles,
cranes' marches
among flowing creeks and
waving willows bent
with sweet ancient reveries
borne on windswept fields,
soft sputtered cries of yearning,
muttered words of intangible longing —
and seek you within,
O Lover,
all the secret nooks known
in childhood's
warm embraces —
soft meadow breezes
and sunset-kissed horizons,
wandered meadows
and the lullabies of seashores,
the rush of first love
and tears rolling down lips
bellowing laughter.
I will not speak of you,
O Love,
in false foreign tongues
which do not spark and glow
with the raw earthiness
from which I have flown,
which do not build

in each syllable of speech
a bridge of light
between hearts and skies.
No.
I will seek you in the well-known
fields and forages of homes
kindling heart-hearths
of love-litanies.
There,
I will meet
You,
and
You,
I.

# *Twilight Medleys*

The lovers' silhouettes are lost
in the shadows of
that great fading light.
Sparkling embers of glory
trail upon the horizon's face,
melting into soft waves —
a song upon the rocks.

*Twilight Medleys | Afna, Morocco | Sunset and two lovers on Plage 'Ain Diab*

# *The Ḥabībiyya*

As we entered Meknes' *El Haboul* district, we were guided by the lilt of a *wird* flowing sweetly, softly, like a soft summer breeze. The words were indiscernible at first, but as we approached the open portal of the *zāwiya*, they became lucid and pronounced. It was a poem from the renowned *dīwān* of *Shaykh* Muḥammad ibn al-Ḥabīb. We stepped through the open door and entered the sanctum.

"*As-salāmu 'alaykum.* Peace be with you."

The chanting ceased.

"*Wa 'alaykum as-salām wa raḥmatu-Llāhi wa barakatuh.* And may the peace, mercy, and blessings of God be upon you," the man in the *zāwiya* replied, "*Marḥaba, marḥaba!* Welcome, welcome!"

The living, blind *walī, Sīdī* 'Alī, welcomed us warmly. He invited us to join him on the sofa near the entrance. Before joining him, we stood solemnly before the tomb of the *Shaykh* and offered a supplication. We were promptly offered tea and we joined *Sīdī* 'Alī on the sofa. He smiled graciously while running his fingers through his prayer beads. Without hesitation, he returned to his recitation of the *dīwān*, his lips and heart occupied with familiar praise. We had returned to a second home, the *zāwiya* of *Shaykh* Muḥammad ibn al-Ḥabīb.

*Shaykh* Muḥammad ibn al-Ḥabīb was a prominent Moroccan *shaykh*, teacher, and scholar of the twentieth century. He was a master of the *Darqāwī ṭarīqa*, an influential order in Moroccan history and the way of many famous Moroccan spiritual masters including *Moulay* al-'Arabī al-Darqāwī and *Sīdī* Aḥmad ibn 'Ajība. The *Darqāwiyya*, a branch of the *Shādhilī ṭarīqa*, spread across Morocco and the region. Though he was a recent master, passing away to his Lord in 1972, *Shaykh* Muḥammad ibn al-Ḥabīb embodied the fullness of the Moroccan path of Sufism. After his studies and travels across the Islamic world, he established a *Darqāwī zāwiya* in Meknes, where he continued his teachings. His legacy and teachings would serve as the foundation for another branch of the *ṭarīqa* continued by his students and successors, the *Darqāwiyya-Ḥabibiyya.*

The *Darqāwiyya-Ḥabībiyya zāwiya* of Meknes was, and still is, a welcoming hub for many of the foreign spiritual seekers who visit Morocco. For the many Muslim students studying Arabic in Fes, visiting the *zāwiya* in Meknes, a journey often made by hitchhiking with a band of singing *Darqāwī fuqarā'*, is a regular and cherished ritual. While we would visit many of Meknes' *awliyā'* regularly, we always began our visits with the *zāwiya* of *Shaykh* Muḥammad ibn al-Ḥabīb. As one of the greatest gnostics of the Moroccan tradition, he inspired many wayfarers from around the world.

During his many decades of service, *Shaykh* Muḥammed ibn al-Ḥabīb encountered and attracted many Westerners drawn to the path of *taṣawwuf.* Through the guidance and teaching of the *Shaykh*, Sufism spread rapidly to and in the West. The *zāwiya* is still a crossroads between East and West, hosting *murīdūn* from as far as the United States and Indonesia. The *Shaykh's* influence continues to resonate today; his *zāwiya* is still a physical and spiritual home to many visitors who thirst for a quenching drink from the wells of *taṣawwuf.*

The *baraka* of the *zāwiya* was undeniably sensed upon entrance. Visitors often described a cool and soothing wave of peace flooding upon them. One was always greeted by *Sīdī* 'Alī, the radiant and tranquil blind *walī* of Meknes. *Sīdī* 'Alī lived in the *zāwiya* for many years and was often found resting beside the tomb of his master. He engaged in constant remembrance — singing *qasā'id* from the *Shaykh's dīwān*, chanting the *wird* of the *Darqāwī* order, or reciting from the Qur'an. One was also welcomed by *Ḥajjah* Zulaykha, one of the *Shaykh's* living wives who remained as the caretaker of the *zāwiya* and its guests until her passing. Meknes is also the home of *Moulay* Hāshim, one of the dedicated students and a living spiritual inheritor of *Shaykh* Muḥammad ibn al-Ḥabīb. His home and heart are always open for those seeking counsel, and he continues to be a light and guide of the way of the *Darqāwiyya.* Meknes is a special home of the *awliyā'*, and each sincere pilgrim discovers a manifest or hidden reward in their visitation.

While Meknes is a pulsing hub of *dhikr* throughout the year, there are special *mawlid* gatherings hosted in the *zāwiya* during *Rabī' al-Awwal.* Dozens of *fuqarāʾ* travel to attend the blessed gatherings. Among all the *fuqarāʾ* who gather from across Morocco, the region, and the world, a deep love and devotion to the *Shaykh* and to the Prophet pulses while the *awrād* are recited, the *qasāʾid* are chanted, and the *ḥaḍra* is performed. Everyone unites in the descending *baraka.* Everyone unites in praise of the One to whom all things return.

Though the *Shaykh* left his physical form, his presence continues, in Meknes and in the world, through the *baraka* of the *zāwiya*, the light of the people he inspired, the presence of his *fuqarāʾ*, and the guidance of *Moulay* Hāshim. The *Ḥabībiyya* continue to carry the traditions of Moroccan Sufism into all corners of the world — keeping tongues and hearts alike alight with praise, supplication, and *dhikr.*

## *Light Upon the Midnight Haze*

The midnight haze has set
upon silent streets broken
by soft rays of streetlamps
and candles roaring in quiet
nooks. Memories of markets
linger in piles of peels and
cats' paws on whispering
windswept steps as scents
of smoke and warmth
drown in the swirling chill
of winter night. Billowing air
tumbles from cracked lips like incense
soaring from rumbling cisterns and twisting
alleys still surprise the wandering strangers
like *koans* emerging from the silence, reminding —
you are masters of nothing but fleeting moments.
Yet, hidden in the city labyrinth's unfolding maps
of stone and wood, souls bound in the soft
robes of love illuminate dark corners,
prayers pour from hearts enamored,
rapt like birds soaring in the morning skies.
Here, we recall primordial promises, reminding —
you are masters of a precious moment,
and we are nourished
until the morning call.

## *Burning*

The loss of memory
of primal unity
and the entanglement of essences
obscure
the inner mirror
to the dance of cosmic light
within
as the spreading flames
of self glow, faintly, seeping
a burning chasm,
a rift —
the soft bleedings of the soul
yearning for the polishing
of the mirror of the heart.

# *Dew Drops of Morning Nectar*

Birds,
  sirens of the rising sun
at the pooling nectars of dawn,
      emerge from the wombs
of the waking earth.
   Warbles, hymns
      in a language beyond
  the reach of the ear,
sound the beginnings
   of a new day
   of perpetual emergence:
                dawn
                    light
                        birthright.

# *Solitude*

A solitary tree graces a field in southern Morocco. Its shade provides the only solace for travelers on the road. Under its thin branches, one can sit in silence and absorb the rhythms of the earth and birdsong. Here, the earth and sun are the great timekeepers. In its solemn and dignified stillness, this tree roots itself in sacred time.

*Solitude | Plains outside of the village of Oukeet | Oukeet, Morocco | Rolling plains en route to a farm*

# *Enchanted*

How can I be anything other than
enchanted,
engulfed
in every bursting blessing
hidden
within the streams
of hours and days
of songs and dances
of revelations borne
on every breath?

# *Return*

Your forehead pushes into the cold, soft sand. Your hands slip between the silky waves as your fingernails dig deep. In this Saharan submission, your indelible roots in the earth are recalled with great, crushing freshness. Your prayer will be absorbed into the earth, into the sand. In this world, its traces vanish. It belongs to a different order of time, a different way of being. It is the journey of return to primal unity.

*Return | The dunes of Merzouga | Merzouga, Morocco | Morning supplications in the soft sand*

# *Ascent*

Ascent
    is never direct.
    It is gradual,
        imperceptible,
the erosions
    of thick
     and stony hearts
    by the vibrations of the
            Most Subtle
                        *Yā Laṭīf*[7]
            Most Gentle
                        *Yā Laṭīf.*

Grief fades
in the rolling streams of mercy
flowing to the sea and shore
    beyond.

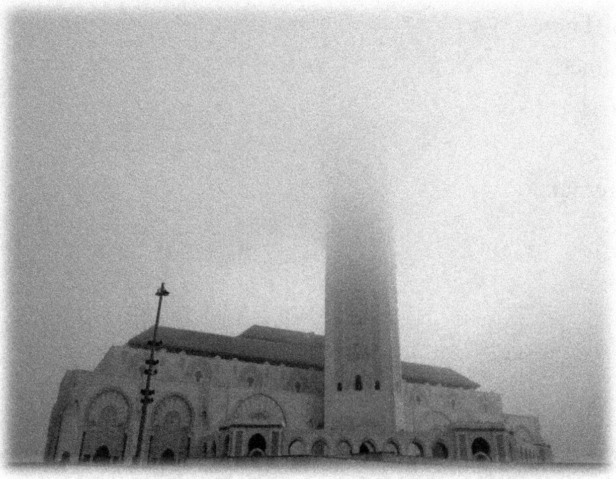

[7] *Al-Laṭīf,* the Most Gentle, the Most Subtle, is one of the ninety-nine names of God in the Islamic tradition.

# *Cascade*

Moments
seeping transcendence
cascade,
too much
light
for eyes
to hold,
for hearts
to bear,
descending,
showering,
flowing
as gushing springs
in hours
of nearness
folded within
caresses of
the Beloved. There
where fullness
springs
anew,
eternal.

# *The Living Walī*

Gentle, cool breezes wafted through the *medīna* alleys, a welcome reprieve from the late-summer heat of the northern plains. Ramadan had finished and the city resumed its daily routines. Several friends, brothers and sisters of the *Naqshbandi ṭarīqa* and students of the beloved *Shaykh* Nazim al-Haqqani, visited for the summer. We walked through the shuttered and sleepy *medīna* to the Qarawiyyīn *masjid*, where all assembled for the Friday sermon and prayers. The Qarawiyyīn was a special, blessed center for most *Fāsīs*.

"All roads lead to the Qarawiyyīn. It is the heart of our city. Fes mirrors the heavens. It is impossible to be unmindful of God; there are reminders on every street and in every corner. But, if you want to know our life source, go to the heart," a local *shaykh* once shared.

The flowing, spring-fed fountains pulsed with brisk water as worshipers meticulously completed their prescribed ablutions. The *adhān* sounded, followed by the Friday sermon. Everyone sought out a place to sit on the *masjid* carpets. We assembled as a group and offered our petitions and supplications in unison.

After the prayer, we sat in contemplation for some time before turning to the back of the *masjid*, where the sound of melodious chanting could be heard, first faintly, and then in gentle crescendo. We spotted a crowd of visitors sitting in a circle on the floor, swaying to the recitation. We joined the group quietly, seeking not to disturb the invocations, and joined the recitation.

After the Friday communal prayer, *Shaykh* Ayashi, a reserved, tranquil old man, remained in the back of the Qarawiyyīn mosque of Fes. He was silent, serene, and surrounded by his sons, grandsons, and visitors who sought his prayers and blessing. His face, bent towards the earth in reverence, was easily spotted through the passing crowds. He sat long after the prayer has ended, busy with *dhikr* and the recitation of the *Dalā'il al-Khayrāt* which, like many *Fāsīs*, he had memorized in full in his youth. He swayed in perfect unison to the words etched upon his heart and tongue. His name was well-known among the people of Fes, and he was known as one of the last living *awliyā'* of the city.

*Shaykh* Ayashi was once a herdsman and a farmer in the fields outside of Fes. According to many *Fāsīs,* the *Shaykh* was over the age of 120. Like most elder Moroccans, no birth certificate was recorded. Though he was illiterate, he had memorized the Qur'an and the *Dalā'il al-Khayrāt,* reciting these texts throughout the day with constant prayer and attention to God and His Prophet. He was a *shaykh* of the *Jazūlī ṭarīqa,* one of the most important Sufi orders of Morocco. Though he was blind and could no longer walk, he was known to be highly perceptive, sensing objects and events around him despite his lack of physical vision. He was visited in his home regularly by neighbors, students, *shuyūkh,* local and international scholars, and visitors seeking the living, pulsing *baraka* of the city. They brought gifts and prayer requests, and they left with *baraka* and a full heart. Many do not pass his corner of the *medīna* of Fes without visiting his home.

In constantly reciting the *Dalā'il al-Khayrāt,* the *Shaykh* embodied the greatest legacy of *Imām* al-Jazūlī and the Moroccan school of Sufism — sending constant prayers and blessings upon the Prophet Muhammad and his family and companions. The virtues of remembrance, devotion, constancy, and attention in seeking perfect submission is the aim of the great Sufi masters. These virtues continue to thrive in the world through silent, hidden *awliyā'* like this *Shaykh.* Through his devotion to the messengers and prophets of God, he fulfilled his quest to emulate them in God-consciousness. He was a pillar of these spiritual traditions in an age marked by forgetfulness, arrogance, and greed.

In his silent devotion, he cultivated a shimmering light which is shared with those visitors of pure intention and aspiration. Those who drank from this well left the presence of the *Shaykh* with a sense of deep, enduring peace. Before his recent passing, he was one of the living patron saints of Fes, the last of a noble generation of scholars and saints. It is said that the angels protected him in his old age, sustaining his wisdom and presence in the world — his continued presence, according to his followers, was a gift and mercy from God, a reminder to live a life of complete and selfless submission to the Lord of the worlds. With him resided the results of wayfaring, and with him the ideals of the spiritual paths were encountered in renewed freshness and joy.

After we completed a partial recitation of the *Dala'il al-Khayrāt* together, the *Shaykh* conferred his blessing upon the group. He left slowly and quietly with his children, returning home to rest for the afternoon. We drank from the well of living light, and left the Qarawiyyīn with that famed, deep, and sustained peace.

## *Awakening*

The moment comes, an
 awakening
  to primordial litanies,
the way of becoming
  glowing
as spreading beams of moonlight
  upon the morning mists —
                                        remember,
                                                remember,
                                                        remember.

## *Time*

How is a moment, often encountered as a fleeting wave of an inundating, swirling ocean, measured? To the mindful, each moment is rooted in the Eternal. Sacramental perception pierces beyond the veils of limitation, corruption, and disunity. The memory of Divine Unicity invokes our primal source, pointing to the depth of each moment — *lā ilāha illa Allāh.*

*Time | A clock adorning a wall in the tomb of Imām al-Jazūlī | Marrakesh, Morocco*

# *Love*

Love
  stirs in all things
first
  as quiet echoes
    ringing,
      remembered
  in the golden
    glimmering
mists
      and soft visions
        of dreams,
      a wondrous
        infatuation with all things
  beautiful,
all things
          ineffably sacred, then
    it bursts
        in instants
 sudden
  and nurtured
from those great
  vaulted
      mysterious
          ancestral
            depths
              of the heart
  and,
in the wake
  of its rush
    upon all things
      vast
        and weak,
        ablution's hymns resound.

In those whispered depths,
the pillars
  of the worlds
are found
    to rest.

## *Supplication of Longing*

O Lord,
make me
an instrument
of Your peace,
a reflection
of Your love,
and an embodiment
of Your wisdom.
May Your blessings,
and may Your peace,
and may Your mercy
descend upon
all creation,
especially the oppressed
and those most in need
of Your love.
Through our toils
and through our labors,
may we build the City of God
and the Kingdom of Heaven
in each step,
and word,
and breath.

*Amin.*

## *Wanderer*

The wanderer is lost
in thought, robed
in visions rich
on pathless paths
and roads paved
in dreamscapes drenched
in yearnings
for the Beloved,
beyond the dense mirages
cloaked in beloveds,
discovered,
rediscovered,
embraced
in each moment.

## *The Tijāniyya*

In the heart of Fes *medīna*, *murīdūn* were beginning to gather in the *zāwiya* of *Shaykh* Aḥmad al-Tijānī. The *adhān* for the late afternoon prayer had sounded, and the daily communal reading of the *wird* would soon commence. Men and women clad in an array of brilliantly colored robes clamored through the narrow *medīna* streets, past mule-drawn carts and frolicking children. They filed through the immense, ornate doors of the *zāwiya* and separated into the segregated areas for men and women.

The *zāwiya* was warm, the air rich and heavy with the scent of incense. A few solitary *murīdūn* sat before the tomb of the *Shaykh* Aḥmad al-Tijānī in contemplation and prayer. Most, however, were gathered near the front, where the recitation of the *wird* was well underway. The unified voice sang a well-known and common supplication, the *Ṣalāt al-Fātiḥ,* a jewel of the *Tijānī* tradition:

*"O God, send prayers upon our master Muhammad, the opener of what was closed, and the seal of what had preceded, the helper of the truth by the Truth, and the guide to Your straight path. May God send prayers upon his family according to his greatness and magnificent rank."*

The voices rang deeply, the walls reverberating with cries of love and devotion. The supplication, the heart of the *Tijānī wird,* is said to contain many hidden, unfathomable blessings. It unites the *murīdūn* around the world, connecting them to their *shaykh*, who lived and was buried in Fes, to the beloved Prophet Muhammad, and to their Creator. From this *zāwiya*, from this humble corner of the Fes *medina*, an *axis mundi* roots the world.

The *Tijānī zāwiya* is a pulsing spiritual pole of the city of Fes, always open and always illuminated by the prayers and remembrance of visitors and students. Many *Fāsīs* and *Tijānī* disciples claim that the crumbling state of the *medīna* is a veil protecting the *zāwiya* of *Shaykh* Aḥmad al-Tijānī from all who are insincere, preserving the spiritual inheritance of the city for those blessed with perception, humility, and pure intention. Where some see a decaying, crumbling city, others see a font of spiritual wisdom and radiant Divine presence.

The *Tijānī ṭarīqa* is one of the largest Sufi orders in the world and is particularly influential in West Africa. *Shaykh* Aḥmad al-Tijānī, an 18th century Algerian *shaykh*, was a descendent of the Prophet Muhammad through *Moulay* Idrīs, the patron saint and founder of Fes. He is considered one of the greatest gnostics of the Sufi tradition. Born into a scholarly family, *Shaykh* al-Tijānī excelled in his studies and mastered the religious sciences at an early age. The *Shaykh* settled in Fes, the religious and intellectual capital of the region during his age. He took from many spiritual and intellectual masters of North Africa. After much training, he was blessed with a direct, waking vision of the Prophet Muhammad. The Prophet gave *Shaykh* Aḥmad al-Tijani the *wird* of the *ṭarīqa*. This *wird* is treasured by the *Tijānī murīdūn*, and it is recited daily, individually and communally, by most disciples. The *Shaykh* returned to Fes and, by order of the Prophet, began constructing the *Tijānī zāwiya* in 1800.

The *zāwiya* remains today and serves as a constant house of remembrance, preserving and maintaining the gnostic way of *Shaykh* Aḥmad al-Tijānī. The *wird* of the order is recited in unison three times a day, and at all other times by individual disciples. The *zāwiya* creates enduring ties of pilgrimage and exchange between North and West Africa, hosting disciples from every corner of the world. In a time when Sufi traditions are disappearing, the *zāwiya* of *Shaykh* Aḥmad al-Tijānī remains as a protected well of the wisdom of *taṣawwuf* in the land of saints. The *zāwiya* is a beating heart of the city, pulsing with the enduring and unceasing presence and *baraka* of *Shaykh* Aḥmad al-Tijānī and his inheritors.

مَا رَأَيْتُ إِلّا جَمِيلًا

Naught saw I save beauty.

*Zaynab bint ʿAlī*

# *Glossary*

*Adab*: manners; courtesy

*Adhān*: the call to prayer

*Adhkār*: see *dhikr*

*Alhamdulillāh*: an Arabic phrase for "praise be to God," often uttered in thanksgiving

*Amazigh*: Berber

*Awliyā'*: see *wali*

*Awrād:* see *wird*

*Baraka*: blessedness; Divine presence

*Dalā'il al-Khayrāt*: an important collection of prayers and benedictions upon the Prophet Muhammad from the Moroccan tradition composed by Imam al-Jazūlī in the 15th century

*Ḍarīḥ*: tomb of a saint

*Dhikr (pl. adhkār)*: an Arabic term for "remembrance;" a Sufi spiritual practice often offered in the form of a private or communal litany

*Dīwān*: a collection of poetry

*Du'a' al-Nāṣiriyya:* an important invocation of the Moroccan Sufi tradition composed by *Shaykh* Muḥammad ibn Nāṣir in the 17th century

*Fajr:* the early-morning prayer

*Faqīr (pl. fuqarā')*: literally "one who is in need;" a term accorded to the disciples of a Sufi path and/or the students of a *shaykh*

*Fiṭra*: primordial human nature, rooted in knowledge of God's Oneness

*Fiqh*: the science of religious law and jurisprudence; deep and holistic comprehension and understanding

*Fuqarā'*: see *faqīr*

*Ḥaḍra*: a collective ritual performed by many Sufi orders which involves bodily movement and the recitation of mystical poetry; sometimes referred to as "the sacred dance"

*Ḥajjah*: an honorary term for older and respected women

*Ḥānūt*: a small shop which usually stocks daily goods

*Ḥarīra*: a traditional Moroccan soup with regional variations

*Hillula*: the annual festival celebrating the life of a Jewish saint

*'Ilm*: knowledge

*'Ishā'*: the nighttime prayer

*Jellāba*: a traditional Moroccan robe

*Jennah*: paradise

*Kasbah:* a fortress and defensive structure

*Madrasa:* a traditional religious school

*Maghrib*: the sunset prayer

*Masājid*: see *masjid*

*Masjid (pl. masājid)*: mosque

*Maqsura*: a metal or timber screen used in *masājid* and homes for protection and privacy

*Mawlid*: a celebration of the birth of the Prophet Muhammad; occurs annually during the Islam month of *Rabī' al-Awwal*

*Medīna:* city or urban center; often used to refer to a traditional urban space.

*Moulay*: a term of respect reserved for the *awliyā'* and *shuyūkh* in the context of Moroccan Sufism

*Muqaddam*: the representative of a Sufi *shaykh* or the caretaker of a shrine, tomb, or *zāwiya*

*Murīd (pl. murīdūn)*: literally "a seeker;" a term accorded to the disciples of a Sufi path and/or the students of a *shaykh*

*Murīdūn*: see *murīd*

*Moussem*: festival; the annual festival celebrating the life of a *walī*

*Qasā'id:* see *qasīda*

*Qasīda (pl. qasā'id)*: song or poem

*Qasīdat al-Burda*: "Poem of the Mantle," a poem of praise for the Prophet Muḥammad composed by Muḥammad al-Būṣīrī, a famous Sufi of Egypt, in the 13th century

*Qubba:* the domed tomb of a saint

*Riaḍ*: an Arabic term for "garden;" a term for the traditional Moroccan home centered around an interior garden or courtyard

*Ṣalāt al-Mashīshiyya*: an important invocation of the Moroccan Sufi tradition; composed by *Shaykh* Abd al-Salām ibn Mashīsh in the 12th century.

*Shaykh (pl. shuyūkh)*: spiritual guide often associated with a Sufi order; a general term for a respected elder

*Shurafā':* descendants of the Prophet Muhammad, according highly valued social honor in Moroccan society

*Shuyūkh:* see *shaykh*

*Sīdī*: an honorific title for men; used commonly in Sufi circles

*Simorgh*: a creature in Persian mythology and a common symbol in classical Persianate Sufi poetry; figures prominently in the 12th century *Conference of the Birds* by Sufi poet Farīd al-Din 'Attar

*Ṭarīqa (pl. ṭuruq)*: Sufi order

*Taṣawwuf*: Sufism

*Tasbiḥ*: Islamic prayer beads

*Ṭuruq:* see *ṭarīqa*

*Tziddiq (pl. Tziddiqim):* Jewish saint

*Tziddiqim:* See *tziddiq*

*Walī (pl. awliyā'):* saint

*Wird (pl. awrād)*: Sufi litany

*Zawāyā*: see *zāwiya*

*Zāwiya (pl. zawāyā)*: Sufi lodge or gathering place

*Zillīj*: traditional Moroccan tile work

*Ziyāra*: visitation to a tomb or holy place

سُبحانَ رَبِّكَ رَبِّ العِزَّةِ عَمّا يَصِفونَ ﴿١٨٠﴾

وَسَلامٌ عَلَى المُرسَلينَ ﴿١٨١﴾

وَالحَمدُ لِلَّهِ رَبِّ العالَمينَ ﴿١٨٢﴾

Exalted is your Lord, the Lord of glory, above what they describe; peace be upon the messengers and praise be to God, the Lord of the worlds.[8]

*Qur'ān: 37:180-182*

[8] A Qur'anic verse which is commonly used to conclude prayers and supplications.

CPSIA information can be obtained
at www.ICGtesting.com
Printed in the USA
LVHW020939260521
688448LV00011B/847

9 781916 248830